T0272709

Before using these books...

☞ A teacher/counselor manual is separately available for guiding students in the use of these workbooks.

✐ To prevent bleed-through, it is recommended that water-based, rather than spirit-based, markers or pens be used in this workbook.

Important

This book is not intended as a treatment tool or to be utilized for diagnostic or investigative purposes. It is not designed for and should not be recommended or suggested for use in any unsupervised, self-help or self-therapy setting, group or situation. Professionals who use this book are exercising their own professional judgement and take full responsibility for doing so.

The STARS LifeSkills Program

Teacher/Counselor Manual

Learning About Anger

Learning More About Anger

Knowing Yourself

Getting Along with Others

Respecting Others

How Drugs and Alcohol Affect Us

Getting Along with Others

Jan Stewart
Illustrated by Cecilia Bowman
ISBN 978-1-63026-832-9

© 2003 Jan Stewart and Hunter House
Design and layout Jinni Fontana © 2003 Hunter House
First U.S. edition published in 2003 by Hunter House.

For further information, contact Hunter House, Inc.

STARS: Steps to Achieving Real-life Skills

Getting Along with Others

Dear Student:

This workbook is part of a program to help you learn some real-life skills. You may already have some of these skills, and the information may just be a reminder or a review. If the information is new to you, then it is possible for you to learn skills and strategies that can help you for the rest of your life.

If you are unable to complete any section, leave it blank and come back to it later. If you are still unsure, ask your parent or guardian to assist you. If this is not possible, ask the person who gave you the workbook. On the next page there is a glossary of words that are used in the workbook. Read this before you begin.

Please remember to have your parent or guardian fill out the last page.

Thank you for your cooperation.

Name of Student: _____

Adviser: _____

Assignment Date: _____

Completion Date: _____

Glossary

Characteristic—a feature or quality

Consequence—the result of something

Cruelty—making someone else suffer or hurt

Discrimination—treating someone unfairly due to prejudice based on race, color, or sex

Intimidation—frightening or threatening someone

Jealousy—being afraid or resentful of another person's abilities, or possessive of another person

Manage—feel in control of something, handle something well

Manipulation—taking advantage of someone by controlling them in unfair ways.

Violence—use of force that can injure or abuse

The STARS LifeSkills Program ★ Getting Along with Others ©2003 Jan Stewart and Hunter House, Inc.

Getting Along with Others

Getting along with others is a skill that can be learned. People who don't get along with others are often aggressive. Many people are not aware that they are aggressive. Some people hurt others to feel powerful. It's all right to have power, but it isn't all right to hurt others. Sometimes people need to find another response that will allow them to get what they want while respecting themselves and others. And everyone could use help becoming a better friend. This work book is divided into two parts: in Part One you will learn about what bullying is and how to deal with anger; in Part Two you will learn more about being a good friend.

Part One: All About Bullying

Many words may be used to describe the way people act inappropriately toward others. Taunting, harassing, victimizing, and bullying are the most common terms that will be dealt with in this unit. The person causing harm will be called the bully. The other person will be called the victim.

Using your dictionary, look up the following words:

1. Taunt _____

2. Harass _____

3. Victimize _____

4. Bully _____

5. Annoy _____

Bullying Hurts People

We can't always see what's going on inside of others. Even if they look tough on the outside, they may have very different feelings on the inside. Every now and then, put yourself in someone else's shoes. How would you feel if you were the victim?

_____

_____

_____

The STARS LifeSkills Program ★ Getting Along with Others ©2003 Jan Stewart and Hunter House, Inc.

What Does a Victim Look Like?
What Does a Bully Look Like?

Draw a picture of a bully and a victim.

BULLY

VICTIM

What would you expect a bully to say when bullying someone?

_____

_____

_____

_____

What would you expect a victim to say when being bullied?

_____

_____

_____

_____

Remember:

Many bullies are also victims in another environment.

The STARS LifeSkills Program ★ Getting Along with Others ©2003 Jan Stewart and Hunter House, Inc.

Understanding Bullies and Victims

What words come to your mind when you hear the word BULLIES?

_____   _____

_____   _____

_____   _____

What do you think are some characteristics of people who bully others?

_____   _____

_____   _____

_____   _____

What do you think are some characteristics of people who get bullied?

_____   _____

_____   _____

_____   _____

Make a list of the characteristics you believe you have—use either list or choose your own words.

_____   _____

_____   _____

_____   _____

Bullying involves using power and aggression to control another person. Aggression may be physical, emotional, or verbal. Below are examples of aggression. **Add at least two more examples of your own to each list.**

Physical:

hitting, shoving, throwing objects

_____   _____

_____   _____

_____   _____

Emotional:

ignoring, laughing at someone, lying

_____   _____

_____   _____

_____   _____

Verbal:

put downs, threats, teasing

_____   _____

_____   _____

_____   _____

Bullying is a form of violence and is a serious offense.
Many victims are seriously hurt by how they are treated by bullies.

The STARS LifeSkills Program ★ Getting Along with Others ©2003 Jan Stewart and Hunter House, Inc.

Responding to Anger

Aggressive anger:	Involves demanding your rights without thinking about the rights of others.
	This type of anger hurts people either emotionally, physically, or psychologically.
Aggressive people...	Blame others.
	Use physical or verbal violence.
	Bully or push people around.
	Yell or scream at others.
Passive anger:	Involves keeping your anger inside, and not dealing with the issue.
	This anger could result in feeling like you want to get even.
	Examples of passive anger include not talking to the other person, spreading rumors, and damaging people's property.
Passive people...	Make excuses.
	Don't want to express themselves.
	Blame themselves.
Assertive anger:	Involves standing up for your own rights and, at the same time, respecting the rights of others.
	This type of anger is expressed directly and in a non-threatening way to the other person involved.
Assertive people...	Use a variety of techniques to respond to anger.
	Express their feelings and thoughts to others.
	Are honest with themselves and others

Which type of response do you think someone who is bullying has to anger?
Which type of response do you think someone who is a victim has?

The STARS LifeSkills Program ★ Getting Along with Others ©2003 Jan Stewart and Hunter House, Inc.

Body Language

Body language is the way a person communicates with others without using words. Below are examples of how the three types of people might behave.

Aggressive	Passive	Assertive

Aggressive

- putting hands on the waist or fold them across chest
- speaking loudly
- acting like they are better than others
- narrowing or squinting eyes
- staring
- pointing fingers
- clenching fists
- crowding others' personal space

Passive

- speaking softly
- looking down, making little eye contact
- clearing throat
- laughing when expressing anger
- acting anxious
- stepping back from others
- pleading with people

Assertive

- acting as if they are equal to others
- making good eye contact
- speaking with a clear and positive voice
- leaning slightly forward when talking to others
- respecting others' personal space

Using the information you now have about the personality types of certain people, **draw what each might look like.**

Aggressive

Passive

Assertive

Thinking Straight

How do you rate yourself? **For each pair of statements, check the box on the right or left that seems to represent the way you usually think.**

☐ Everything should always go my way.	☐ To be fair, things should go my way half the time, and the other person's way the other half the time.
☐ I don't care if I hurt other people	☐ I feel bad if I hurt other people because I know how it feels to be hurt.
☐ Success should come easily and quickly, or I'll quit.	☐ I know that success takes hard work and a lot of time.
☐ I shouldn't have to follow rules or do boring things.	☐ I have to follow the rules and do my chores like everyone else.
☐ Lying can keep you out of trouble.	☐ Lying is the wrong thing to do.
☐ I never make mistakes and things are never my fault.	☐ Everyone makes mistakes and things are probably my fault about half the time
☐ Most kids my age are boring and always pleasing adults.	☐ I have a lot in common with kids my age.

The STARS LifeSkills Program ★ *Getting Along with Others* ©2003 Jan Stewart and Hunter House, Inc.

Now think about how someone else might see you. Think of a teacher, a parent, or a student. How do you think they see you? How would they guess you think? If you want to take a chance, you could give them the following statements to see how they think you would answer.

☐ Everything should always go my way.

☐ To be fair, things should go my way half the time, and the other person's way the other half the time.

☐ I don't care if I hurt other people

☐ I feel bad if I hurt other people because I know how it feels to be hurt.

☐ Success should come easily and quickly, or I'll quit.

☐ I know that success takes hard work and a lot of time.

☐ I shouldn't have to follow rules or do boring things.

☐ I have to follow the rules and do my chores like everyone else.

☐ Lying can keep you out of trouble.

☐ Lying is the wrong thing to do.

☐ I never make mistakes and things are never my fault.

☐ Everyone makes mistakes and things are probably my fault about half the time

☐ Most kids my age are boring and always pleasing adults.

☐ I have a lot in common with kids my age.

How was what you said about yourself the same or different from how you think others see you?

_____

_____

_____

The STARS LifeSkills Program ★ Getting Along with Others ©2003 Jan Stewart and Hunter House, Inc.

Put a check beside the way you think most of the time.

Crooked (Incorrect) Thinking	Straight (Correct) Thinking
☐ If something goes wrong, it's not my fault. Someone else makes me act badly.	☐ I am responsible for my behavior.
☐ When I don't want to do something I say, "I can't."	☐ "I can't" really means "I won't" and that is a choice that has consequences.
☐ I don't hurt other people. They exaggerate being upset to get me in trouble.	☐ My behavior can hurt others, including their feelings.
☐ I don't care how other people feel or if I hurt them.	☐ I don't want to hurt others because I don't like feeling hurt.
☐ I hate having to work hard or do boring tasks, so I try to avoid them.	☐ Life is not all fun and games; sometimes you have to do boring or difficult tasks.
☐ I hate obligations, rule, and "must do's," so I refuse or ignore them.	☐ Everyone should play by the rules and fulfill his or her obligations.
☐ I watch out for myself and always try to get my way.	☐ An attitude of fairness and a "give and take" balance must exist in good relationships.
☐ I don't trust other people and they don't trust me.	☐ Trust must be earned and developed over time.

The STARS LifeSkills Program ★ Getting Along with Others ©2003 Jan Stewart and Hunter House, Inc.

Crooked (Incorrect) Thinking	Straight (Correct) Thinking
☐ I can always be successful at everything.	☐ Success comes from hard work, planning, learning from mistakes, and being a good person.
☐ I make decisions quickly and without even trying.	☐ Good decisions are thought out and based on facts.
☐ I am proud that I never make mistakes.	☐ Everyone makes mistakes, and mistakes help you learn.
☐ I do what I want and figure that the future will take care of itself.	☐ Things work out better if I think about and plan for the future.
☐ I am good at doing things quickly, without even trying.	☐ Success takes hard work and comes in stages.
☐ I get really upset if someone says something negative to me or puts me down.	☐ Constructive criticism can help me learn. I want my friends to be honest with me.
☐ I'm never afraid of anything.	☐ Everyone feels fear sometimes and others can help me when I'm afraid.
☐ I get angry when I don't get my way, and sometimes I use anger to get my way.	☐ I am responsible for my feelings and have choices about how I express them.
☐ I like having power because then I can win and get my own way.	☐ Power is earned and should never be used to hurt others.

Thinking About Your Thoughts

Sound confusing? It is a bit. Try thinking about a situation and how you thought about it. This will tell you if you're thinking straight or crooked. Here are a couple of examples:

EXAMPLE 1

Situation: Mika didn't invite me to her birthday party.

My Thoughts: I thought Mika was a snob and I wanted to get back at her.

Was My Thinking STRAIGHT or

CROOKED?

Because: I don't have to be invited to everyone's parties to feel good about myself.

EXAMPLE 2

Situation: I didn't pass my English test, so I crumpled it up and threw it at the teacher's face.

My Thoughts: I thought I was never going to pass this class, and it's the teacher's fault that I failed.

Was My Thinking STRAIGHT or

CROOKED?

Because: Doing well in school is my responsibility and it will take a lot of work.

Example 1

Situation: _____

_____

My Thoughts: _____

_____

Was my thinking   STRAIGHT   or   CROOKED?

Because:_____

_____

Example 2

Situation: _____

_____

My Thoughts: _____

_____

Was my Thinking   STRAIGHT   or   CROOKED?

Because:_____

_____

Always Remember:

You control what you think.

You can make yourself feel good or bad.

You are in charge of how you think and feel.

You decide what kind of person to be.

So You're Angry –What Are You Going to Do About It?

Here are some ideas to help you work through situations that make you angry. The following are called control techniques. To help you remember the techniques, remember the words **ICE CREAM.**

I — Imagine somewhere calm

C — Count backwards

E — Exercise

C — Consequence acceptance

R — Relaxation techniques

E — Either solve it . . . or leave it

A — Assert yourself

M — Music

Imagine Somewhere Calm

Thinking about a nice place can have a pleasant effect on your body. The best part about this is it can be anywhere you want. You might even imagine being somewhere out of this world.

Count Backwards

Counting backwards from twenty slowly can help you get control of yourself. It gives you time to STOP...THINK...THEN ACT. This technique gives you time to think about the best way to act.

Exercise

Exercise like walking, running, skating, or biking can do wonders for your body. Exercise will not only help you calm down if you are already angry, but also it will help prevent you from feeling angry in the first place. When your body is healthy, your mind is healthy. A lot of people feel sad or irritable when they don't exercise daily. Any exercise is better than no exercise. Find a routine that works for you.

The STARS LifeSkills Program ★ Getting Along with Others ©2003 Jan Stewart and Hunter House, Inc.

Consequence Acceptance

Sometimes we make mistakes and there is a logical consequence that follows. In some circumstances, accepting the consequences without becoming discouraged is the best reaction. If you made a mistake, fix it. For example, if you insult someone, apologize.

Relaxation Techniques

Learning to relax is a skill that many people could use. Some common techniques are: taking deep breaths, tensing and then relaxing the different parts of your body, or visualization (imagining yourself in a happy or calm place). Athletes often use this technique before an event to help them relax and concentrate.

Either Solve It...or Leave It

Sometimes, though, the timing just isn't right for problem solving and it might be a better idea to walk away from the situation for a while and come back to it later when you are feeling more ready.

Assert Yourself

There are several methods for being assertive. One of the most common methods is to use an "I" message. An "I" message is an assertive technique used to respond to someone who is trying to provoke you. Here is the formula:

> *When you ...*
>
> *I feel ...*
>
> *because ...*
>
> *I need ...*

Here is how it might sound:

> *When you* take my book,
>
> *I feel* mad
>
> *because* I have to do my work.
>
> *I need* you to give it back.

Here is another example:

> *When you* call me names,
>
> *I feel* hurt
>
> *because* it embarrasses me.
>
> *I need* you to stop insulting me.

Music

Music can help to change your mood. Lively music might make you feel energetic; slower music, on the other hand, might help you calm down. Music can also help to distract some negative feelings and help you put yourself somewhere else that might be more positive.

The STARS LifeSkills Program ★ Getting Along with Others ©2003 Jan Stewart and Hunter House, Inc.

Which Control Techniques Do You Think Would Work for You?

Explain three situations that might make you angry and explain how one of the control techniques would help you. Remember to use the words ICE CREAM to help you remember the techniques.

1. A situation that I would get angry about is . . .

_____

_____

I would use the _____ technique and this is how it would work . . .

_____

_____

2. A situation that I would get angry about is . . .

_____

_____

I would use the _____ technique and this is how it would work . . .

_____

_____

3. A situation that I would get angry about is . . .

_____

_____

I would use the _____ technique and this is how it would work . . .

_____

_____

The STARS LifeSkills Program ★ Getting Along with Others ©2003 Jan Stewart and Hunter House, Inc.

How Do We Stop Bullying?

Using what you have learned so far about anger and bullying, design a poster that would discourage people from bullying others. Include the following: define bullying, examples of bullying, how a victim feels, and how someone can control anger to avoid acting like a bully. Choose any design you wish. It must not promote anything that would hurt someone or something. Use color to make the poster attractive; you may use a separate sheet if needed.

Congratulations! You finished Part One!

You have made a big step towards getting along better with others. In Part Two, you will learn more about something everyone can use brushing up on: how to be a better friend.

Part Two: Being a Better Friend

Being a good friend is a skill that takes practice. In second half of this workbook, you will learn some techniques that will help you to become a better friend.

The STARS LifeSkills Program ★ Getting Along with Others ©2003 Jan Stewart and Hunter House, Inc.

How Friendly Are You?

The STARS LifeSkills Program ★ Getting Along with Others ©2003 Jan Stewart and Hunter House, Inc.

Answer the following statements as honestly as you can. Circle one number using the following scale:

1 = never   2 = sometimes   3 = often   4 = always

1   2   3   4   1. Do you avoid putting other people down?

1   2   3   4   2. Do you compliment (say nice things about) people?

1   2   3   4   3. Do you make other people feel important?

1   2   3   4   4. Do you avoid interrupting when others are talking?

1   2   3   4   5. Are you honest?

1   2   3   4   6. Do you keep secrets and promises?

1   2   3   4   7. Are you a good listener?

1   2   3   4   8. Do you try to imagine what something is like for another person?

1   2   3   4   9. Do you apologize when you hurt someone's feelings?

1   2   3   4   10. Do you comfort others when they are feeling sad or angry?

1   2   3   4   11. Do you encourage others?

1   2   3   4   12. Do you help others feel better when they make a mistake?

1   2   3   4   13. Do you forgive other people when they have made a mistake?

1 2 3 4   14. Do you avoid being jealous when your friend has other friends?

1 2 3 4   15. Do you try to support your friends?

1 2 3 4   16. Do you try to help your friends when they find work difficult?

1 2 3 4   17. Do you enjoy working in groups?

1 2 3 4   18. Are you able to see something good in most people?

1 2 3 4   19. Are people able to count on you?

1 2 3 4   20. Do you get along well with many different types of people?

Scoring

Add up all your points and use the scale on the next page to see how you score.

70–100   You are probably a very supportive and understanding friend. You are probably able to get along with most people. You try very hard to be a good friend.

45–69   You probably are very capable of being an excellent friend. There are likely a few things that you could work on to be an even better friend.

20–44   With some work, you will be able to be a very good friend. There are probably a few areas that you could concentrate on. Based on the checklist, list three of the sentences (by number) that you think would be the easiest for you to improve: #_____, #_____, and #_____.

Review any questions you answered with a 1 or 2. These areas could use some work for you to get along better with others.

The STARS LifeSkills Program ★ Getting Along with Others ©2003 Jan Stewart and Hunter House, Inc.

What is a friend? _____

_____

_____

_____

Do you have a close friend? _____

Did you have a friend who no longer wants to be your friend? _____

Have you had a fight or argument with a friend recently? _____

Now that you have finished the questionnaire, **comment on something that you learned by answering the questions.**

What areas are you good in? _____

_____

_____

What areas do you need to improve on?

_____

_____

_____

Belonging

Everyone has a need to BELONG. If we do not belong to any group, we may feel hurt or unwanted. Sometimes people get confused about how to become part of a group, and they behave in ways that are unacceptable to others. People misbehave for a reason. **There are four main purposes or goals of all such behavior.**

Goal 1 — ATTENTION

Goal 2 — POWER

Goal 3 — REVENGE

Goal 4 — ESCAPE

Try to guess what the goal is of each person in the following four situations.

Situation 1

Tatiana never seems to be serious. During class she is always cracking jokes and the teacher keeps reminding her to be quiet. Tatiana disrupts the class so much that she gets sent out to the hall almost every day.

Why is Tatiana acting this way? Her goal is to get

_____

What are two other ways Tatiana could get this without getting into trouble?

1._____

_____

2._____

_____

The STARS LifeSkills Program ★ Getting Along with Others ©2003 Jan Stewart and Hunter House, Inc.

Situation 2

Anthony sat in his seat with his head down. He hardly ever spoke in class and he didn't have many friends. Once when the teacher asked him a question, he sank in his chair and refused to answer. The teacher asked him over and over again, but he just wouldn't say anything. Finally the teacher gave up and asked another student.

Why is Anthony acting like this? His goal is to

_____

How do you think Anthony feels about himself?

_____

_____

What does Anthony need to make him feel better about himself?

_____

_____

Situation 3

Minh spreads rumors and lies to the girls in her class. Minh intimidates other students because she feels like she has to be the boss of everyone. She doesn't listen to the teacher, and swears whenever she gets mad. Minh has been suspended three times and is in danger of being expelled from school.

What is the goal of Minh's behavior? She wants

_____

What are two other ways in which Minh can be a leader?

1. _____

_____

2. _____

_____

Situation 4

Clarence steals things from students and adults. He's very mean to animals and has been in a lot of fights. On one occasion, a classmate accidentally tripped Clarence and he was embarrassed in front of the whole class. Clarence decided to get the boy back, so he broke into the boy's locker and damaged his books and slashed his sports jacket.

What made Clarence act like this? His goal was to get

_____

What is another way Clarence could have handled this situation?

_____

_____

_____

Situation 5

Peter hates everything about school. He does not seem to fit into any group. He doesn't like sports or any clubs. He used to get As and Bs in all his classes, but now he has Fs in all his classes. His old friends don't want to hang out with him because he never wants to do anything. Lately, he has been sleeping in and missing the mornings at school.

What is Peter's goal?

_____

What do you think might happen to Peter if he doesn't get any support?

_____

_____

_____

The STARS LifeSkills Program ★ Getting Along with Others ©2003 Jan Stewart and Hunter House, Inc.

Negotiation: That's Fair

Ever feel stuck when you have a disagreement? Try to negotiate—meet the other person half way.

Imagine this situation:

Tess and Kenya are very close friends. They made plans to go to a movie on Saturday. At the last minute, Tess was asked by another friend, Leroy, to go to a concert because he won tickets from a radio station. Tess really wanted to go to the concert and she told Kenya that she was going with Leroy. A big argument started and Kenya accused Tess of using her friendship.

It's time for Kenya and Tess to negotiate because that would be fair. **Follow the steps below.**

T   Try to understand what the other person is saying

H   Hear how the other person feels

A   Agree with something the other person says

T'   Tell your side

S   State how you feel

F   Find the main issues

A   Allow discussion of the issues and look for a solution

I   Identify and agree to a solution

R   Review and evaluate the process

T Tess tells Kenya that she understands that they had plans to go to a movie and that it must look like whenever something better comes up, she drops her girlfriends.

H Tess says to Kenya, "You sound really hurt that I'm going to the concert with Leroy."

A Tess may say that she agrees that she's changing sides, and this is very inconvenient.

T' Tess tells Kenya that the concert was a last minute thing and she really wants to see this band, but she couldn't afford a ticket and now that she got a ticket for free, she really wants to go.

S Tess tells Kenya that she feels frustrated and caught in the middle because she values the friendship but at the same time, she's dying to go to the concert with Leroy.

F The main issue seems to be that Kenya feels she's second to Leroy in Tess's eyes.

A Both Tess and Kenya discuss the situation and look for an answer.

I Both friends agree that the best solution is that Tess go to the concert with Leroy, and then Tess and Kenya go to the movie on Sunday and spend the whole day together. They agree that Kenya would probably have done the same thing if she had been in Tess's place.

R Tess and Kenya are still friends and know that in the future they can work things out if something similar happens.

Negotiation and mediation are two effective ways to solve a problem. When both people get what they want and agree on a solution, they both win.

Sometimes negotiation doesn't work because both people are too hurt or angry to listen to each other. They might need a **mediator.** A mediator acts like a referee. A mediator doesn't choose sides; he or she just makes sure that both people have a chance to speak, and that everyone is respectful in the process.

If you are having trouble solving a problem with a friend, you might want to get a trained mediator to help you. Many counselors are trained to do mediation.

Remember that when you negotiate, you need to find solutions that are fair to both people. What are some possible solutions for the following situations?

1. *Raoul's parents want him home at 10:30 P.M., but he knows that the game won't be over until 11 P.M.*

What could be a good solution?

_____

_____

_____

_____

2. *Salana wants to buy a new jacket that costs $98, but she only has $75. Her parents have already given her an allowance for the month.*

What could be a good solution?

_____

_____

_____

_____

Remember:

Getting along well with others takes a lot of work. But with practice, everyone can be a better friend.

Journal Writing–Reflecting

Take a moment to think about the work you have done in this workbook. **Jot down some words about how you felt working on this workbook.** From there, use a sentence starter to write about what you have accomplished. Pick the sentence starter that you like and write a paragraph about anything you want. This is a chance for you to be creative and to write something for yourself. Use the space below and a separate sheet if necessary.

If you are better with pictures, feel free to draw a picture.

Sentence Starters

One time I am not proud of is...

Accepting others is important because...

Being a good friend is...

One thing I am proud of is...

_____

_____

_____

_____

_____

_____

_____

The STARS LifeSkills Program ★ Getting Along with Others ©2003 Jan Stewart and Hunter House, Inc.

Getting Along with Others

Parents/Guardians

It would be helpful if you could review and comment on the work that your child has done in this workbook. We encourage students to work with their parents on certain sections and we thank you for your cooperation. We hope that your child has had a chance to examine their behavior and to plan positively for the future. This unit has exposed students to a lot of information which we hope could be reviewed at home. We greatly appreciate your partnership in this project.

Comments: _____

_____

_____

_____

_____

_____

_____

Please feel free to contact the student's advisor or the person who assigned this workbook if you have any other questions or concerns.

Students

Now that you have completed the workbook, we urge you to provide some comments. Please comment on anything positive, e.g. "What did you like about it?" Also comment on what you did not like. If you have any suggestions, we would also like to hear them. **Congratulations for all your hard work!**

Comments: _____

_____

_____

_____

_____

_____

The STARS LifeSkills Program ★ Getting Along with Others ©2003 Jan Stewart and Hunter House, Inc.